The Tao According to Calvin Coolidge

The Tao According to Calvin Coolidge

Poems by

Charles Rammelkamp

© 2025 Charles Rammelkamp. All rights reserved.
This material may not be reproduced in any form, published,
reprinted, recorded, performed, broadcast,
rewritten, or redistributed without
the explicit permission of Charles Rammelkamp.
All such actions are strictly prohibited by law.

Cover design by Shay Culligan
Cover Image by Gene McCormick
Author photo by Roman Gladstone

ISBN: 978-1-63980-796-3

Kelsay Books
502 South 1040 East, A-119
American Fork, Utah 84003
Kelsaybooks.com

*This book is for my grandchildren,
Paloma and Emilio*

Acknowledgments

Thank you to the following publications, in which versions of these poems previously appeared:

ArLiJo: "Fortinbras Rhymes with FDR"
Fictional Café: "Cab Driver," "First Date," "Grace," "Three or Four Degrees of Emily Dickinson"
Glimpse: "Love Child," "Two Gun"
Meat for Tea: "The Locket," "Silence," "The Tao According to Cal"
Song of the San Joaquin: "Bard"
Trajectory: "The Strike"
The Twin Bill: "The First Lady of Baseball"

"The journey of a thousand miles begins with a single step."

—Lao Tzu

Contents

PRELUDE

Love Match   17

PART ONE

The Notch	21
The Locket	22
The Light	23
More Darkness	24
Ouden	25
No Success Like Failure	26
Three or Four Degrees of Emily Dickinson	27
First Date	28
Grace	30
Marriage	31
Birth	32
Have Faith	33
The Hobby	35

PHILOSOPHICAL INTERLUDE

The Tao According to Cal	39
Silence	40

PART TWO

Boston Police Strike	43
The Strike	45

Vice President	47
President	48
Love Child	50
The Progress of a People	51
Leading Eagle	52
Appointing the First Federal Female Judge	54
Prosperity	55
The Experimental Farm	56

PART THREE

Klan Bake	59
Fathers and Sons	60
Favorite Son	62
I'm Only Sleeping	63
The Path Leading Us Home	64
My Father Dies	65
Losing Grace in the Black Hills	66
Two Gun	68
Cab Driver	70
Robbed of Our Pet	72
I Do Not Choose to Run	74
The Lame Duck	76

PART FOUR

How Can You Tell?	79
Mark of Cain	80
Daddy Death	81
Daddy Burial	83

Guardian	85
In This Silence Discover Yourself	86
The First Lady of Baseball	88
Just a White House Conversation	90
The Return of Two Gun	91
Back in Northampton	93
The Precious Four	95
Thousands of Questions by Hundreds of Reporters	96
Calvin Coolidge Put Together	98
Fortinbras Rhymes with FDR	99
The Good Die Young	101
The Rest Is Silence	102

ENVOI

Bard	105

PRELUDE

Love Match

Big Bill Tilden ruled men's tennis,
six years the reigning amateur champ,
first American to win Wimbledon, in 1920.
My younger brother Calvin and I both admired him,
not that either of us aspired to compete at that level,
but that final day of June we played doubles
against Doctor Joel Boone and James Coupal,
senior physician for the White House.
That's when Calvin injured his toe.

When Boone came back two days later,
for a few more sets with my brother and me and Jim Haley,
Calvin Jr. demurred. "Just a blister,"
he dismissed his injury, but he limped,
burned with a fever, 102.
Boone examined him: the blister the size of his thumbnail,
third toe, behind the second joint.
When the fever mounted, Boone called Coupal.

Father was alarmed. *Oh my beautiful boy:*
I saw it flash across his face, and then it was gone:
fit as Tilden himself, until he wasn't.

The infection entered my brother's blood,
Staphylococcus Aureus, the poison all over.
We took him to Walter Reed,
the finest hospital in the land,
but by then the sepsis had settled in,
an unwanted invader taking over.

Father held his hand, pressing a locket
his own mother had owned
into my brother's palm,
letting him know he'd soon be with our grandmother,
whom we had never known.

Four years later Fleming discovered penicillin.
Though they wouldn't be used widely
until the next world war,
antibiotics could have saved my brother.

PART ONE

The Notch

I'd be sworn in as president in Plymouth Notch
in 1923, almost immediately after President Harding died,
in San Francisco, only 57, his long-suffering wife Florence
reading to him from *The Saturday Evening Post,*
a flattering piece about him.
"That's good. Go on, read some more," his last words
before he convulsed and died.
He'd been ill for about a week.

The Notch is where I was born.
My ancestor, the first John Coolidge,
a Revolutionary War soldier,
owned a farm in Saltash, Windsor County, Vermont,
and with the other settlers renamed Saltash "Plymouth,"
a "citty upon a hill," in honor of the Pilgrims.
Really a necklace of hamlets:
Plymouth Notch, Plymouth Union, Plymouth Kingdom.
John acquired plots of land for his children;
soon enough it swarmed with Coolidges.

People in the Notch were self-reliant,
their speech clean, their lives above reproach.
No mortgages, debts quickly paid.
There was money in the savings bank.
My father? A hard worker, frugal, a politician.
I did my chores, attended the one-room school.

It was a good place to be born; I was lucky.
A good enough place to be buried, too,
when the time comes.

The Locket

When Mother died, only thirty-nine,
the greatest sorrow a boy can suffer
fell over me like a shroud.
I was twelve, going on thirteen, Abbie only ten.
How do you process such grief, except alone?

Mother'd been sick with consumption,
since about the time my sister and I started school.
She stayed home from prayer services,
kept busy with her hands, knitted a counterpane
for me and a hypothetical future bride.
She had so many hopes for my future,
before I was even aware I had one.

When my granddad Calvin Galusha took sick,
he'd had me read to him from the Gospel of John,
and when he died he left me a mare colt and a heifer.
I was nine years old when he died, age sixty-three,
a good life by rural Vermont standards.

But thirty-nine? Even though she'd been sickly,
Mother was way too young to be taken from us.
I took some of her hair, kept it in a locket,
shut up tight with my sadness.

The Light

After Mother died, Aunt Mede—
that's what we called our grandmother —
stepped in to raise me and Abbie,
along with our father.
Aunt Mede and Papa decided to send me
away to Ludlow, to the Black River Academy.

The morning we took the sleigh
for the first trip to school,
the cold bit our faces,
but the ride was like magic
over the Vermont ice,
and I knew I was traveling
out of darkness and into the light.

More Darkness

How I wanted Abbie to join me in Ludlow.
I felt homesick: being on my own was hard.
I didn't play ball or skate or hunt like the other boys.
But I did like oratory, memorized Cicero.
Abbie was just so much more cheerful than me.

I was always more focused on work.
I'd been selling apples and popcorn
at town meetings, in Plymouth Notch,
since I could remember.
Come spring I was out sugaring with all the men.
Papa later told a reporter that I could get
"more sap out of a maple tree than the other boys."

Abbie did come to Black River in 1888,
just before a February blizzard.
She wanted to be a teacher.
But two years later?
In March she got a fever and stomach pains.
Everybody was sure she'd get better.
I was always the delicate one in the family,
Abbie tougher than me by a longshot.
But she died only a few days later,
appendicitis, doctors guessed years later,
but at the time a tragic mystery.

It was just so lonesome in Ludlow without her,
only fifteen when she died.
I'd graduate two months later,
but what was I going to do back in Plymouth Notch,
without my sister there?

Ouden

Six years after Mother passed,
Father started courting the schoolteacher,
Carrie Brown, later named Plymouth Notch postmistress.
I'd known her all my life,
and when they married I felt such relief
he wouldn't be alone in Plymouth
while I was down in Northampton,
starting my studies at Amherst.

Amherst was Black River Academy all over again;
I had difficulty fitting in, making friends,
my shyness like a shroud.
I'd wanted to join a fraternity, but none would have me.
They had a word for men like me—
an ouden. From the Greek word for "nothing."

Eventually, I made my own friends at Amherst.
There was Percy Deering from Saco, Maine.
There was Ernest Hardy from Northampton,
Deering and I roommates at Morse's boardinghouse.

Percy and Ernest, oudens like me, took meals
with the fraternity brothers of Beta Theta Pi,
but when the frat guys approached them about joining,
Percy asked if I could join, too,
and when Dwight Morrow demurred,
calling me an oddball,
Deering declined the invitation,
even though Ernest said yes:
Percy and I stayed proud oudens.

No Success Like Failure

Over my years in college,
I developed my skills
in oratory and debate,
gradually distinguished myself.
Soon enough I'd be someone.

Recognition came by my senior year:
I won the graduation day speaker slot,
the Grove Orator as it was called, a serious honor.
And the speech was a triumph!
I made everybody laugh, again and again.
"The mantle of truth falls upon
the Grove orator only on condition,"
I declaimed, "he wear it wrongside out."
I'd even gotten a nickname, "Cooley."

That's when Phi Gamma Delta asked
Deering and me to join, senior year.
Percy and I did not hesitate.

But still I had problems making progress with women.
Percy's sister, Rose Deering, a student at Smith,
caught my eye, but that romance fizzled fast.
I'd been out of school six years by then,
had run and won for Northampton city council.
I graciously "forgave" Rose when she rejected me,
feeling once again the loser, the "nothing."

Three or Four Degrees of Emily Dickinson

Harvard Law was out—too expensive
($150/year, additional expenses estimated
in the university catalog as up to $471).
But the law was my calling.
What was an Amherst graduate to do?

John C. Hammond, local lawyer, caught my Grove oration
at the 1895 graduation ceremonies,
impressed by my oratorical skills.
When my old ouden friend Ernest Hardy,
who'd joined Beta Theta Pi,
signed up to read law in Northampton
at the offices of Richard Irwin,
he helped me get an interview
at Hammond and Field, another firm
of Amherst men in the county seat,
Hammond already favorably disposed toward me.

Hammond's partner, Henry P. Field,
was family lawyer to Edward Dickinson,
son of the Amherst founder Samuel,
father of Emily and Austin,
Austin the school treasurer, rumored
to have had an affair with an astronomy professor's wife.

Hammond and Field offered me a desk in their shop.
I determined myself to master the law,
qualify as an attorney in three years, maybe two.
I also determined I'd find myself a wife.

First Date

I seemed to be settling in
to the life of a political bachelor:
party meetings, working, holing up in my rooms.
I'd been admitted to the Massachusetts bar in 1897,
been appointed to the Republican City Committee,
been a delegate to the Republican State Convention,
elected a Northampton councilman,
appointed Northampton city solicitor,
Clerk of the Courts for Hampshire County,
but I just didn't know how to meet women.
I was already thirty-two.

Educated women surrounded me—
Smith College was a showcase for them.
Females taught at the Clarke School for the Deaf.
Northampton was crawling with them,
but my shyness overcame me,
and I devoted myself to my legal and political work.

One morning when I was shaving,
my hat on my head as I held the razor,
I heard a peal of laughter, like birdsong,
coming through the window of my Round Hill Road home.
My housemate, Bob Weir, told me
the laughter came from a Clarke School teacher
who'd seen me while watering flowers on the lawn
outside her dormitory across the way.

Grace Anna Goodhue, almost seven years my junior,
sent me a pot of flowers the next day,
and I sent her my calling card.
Our first date?
A political rally at Northampton City Hall.

Grace

One of my friends, Alfred Pearce Dennis,
a teacher at Smith who also lodged in Round Hill Road,
called Grace "a creature of spirit, fire and dew,"
stunned she favored me, a quiet lawyer.
I savored my good fortune, too.

Grace and I were like yin and yang,
she dark, me fair; I hated sports,
she liked to skate, dance, play baseball;
Grace knitted, sewed, crocheted, but
I was no good at any handiwork.
But opposites attract; soon we were inseparable.
We were both Vermonters in Northampton.

Suddenly I was going to events and places
I'd have skipped before, even went ice-skating.
I took her up to Mount Tom on the west bank
of the Connecticut River near Holyoke.
We attended a DAR meeting together at Rahar's Inn,
both of us descendants of revolutionaries,
during Northampton's 250th anniversary.

I took Grace to Plymouth to meet my father and grandmother,
showed her all the beauties of the Green Mountains.
We went to Burlington to see the Goodhues.
By then we'd been intimate for most of a year.

"Up here on some law business, Mr. Coolidge?"
Grace's father, Captain Goodhue asked me.
"Come to see about marrying Grace," I replied.

Marriage

Grace's mother was a tougher nut to crack.
Lemira Goodhue opposed the marriage,
tried to postpone it, advising Grace to wait
until she'd taught at the Clarke School a year,
or learned to bake bread.

"We'll buy our bread," I snapped, losing patience.

Back in Northampton, I ran for the school committee,
but my heart wasn't into it, too distracted by Grace.
Plus, I liked my opponent, John J. Kennedy.
I'd lose the race in December,
but in October, Grace and I married,
a small ceremony in the Goodhues' house,
on Maple Street, in Burlington,
the Congregational Church minister officiating,
me in my Prince Albert double-breasted frock coat,
Grace with her hair done up in a pompadour.
Just fifteen people in attendance,
Father and my grandmother, Aunt Mede, among them.

Alas, Aunt Mede would die
only a few months later, January 2, 1906.
Seems sorrow always mixes with bliss.

Birth

I was 34 when John was born,
a couple of weeks after we moved to Massasoit Street,
just as the clocks struck six on September seventh,
a little less than a year since the wedding,
and two months before my election
to the Massachusetts House of Representatives.

I hated being away, but I loved being a lawmaker,
crafting legislation in the State House on Beacon Hill,
holing up at Adams House on Washington Street,
the dumpy structure by the Western Mass. Club,
those of us who crossed the Connecticut River
to come to Boston.

My 36th birthday still three months away
when we were blessed with Calvin Jr.,
I'd already decided against running for re-election,
concentrating on my law practice instead,
but in 1909 I ran for mayor of Northampton
and won by 107 votes!

Now I could walk to work,
come home to my family,
the first time home had felt so complete
since my mother's death.

Have Faith

Another benefit of being mayor instead of a congressman?
I found executive oversight so much less enervating
than all that legislative horse-trading.

But when my father was elected a Senator for Vermont,
Grace and I traveling to Montpelier to celebrate,
I realized I wanted to go back to Boston,
even though I won re-election in Northampton,
so a couple of years later I ran for State Senate.

I'd always noticed this pattern:
every time I had success,
something humbling darkened my joy.
Abbie'd died my senior year at Black River;
Aunt Mede, my grandmother, had died
right after Grace and I got married.

This time? Just as I prepared
for my triumphant return to Boston as Senate president,
my wee five-year-old boy Calvin Jr. got pneumonia.
We checked him into Northampton General,
doctors removing fluid from his lungs with a needle.

My God, how desperate I felt!
What a relief when the crisis passed!
I went to Boston two weeks later, rose to speak,
the new president of the State Senate,
echoing Demosthenes, whom I'd studied
all those years ago at Amherst:

"Men do not make laws. They do but discover them."
My "Have Faith in Massachusetts" speech
made national headlines!

The Hobby

A reporter once asked me
if I had any hobbies.

"Holding office," I deadpanned in response.
I ran for something seventeen times in my life,
and that doesn't even include the primaries.

Massachusetts elections held every year,
I ran three times for Lieutenant Governor—
1915, 1916, 1917—
running alongside Sam McCall,
my western Mass. constituency
balancing his Boston base.
Sam lived in Winchester, narrowly lost in 1914.

A lieutenant governor doesn't do much,
not even preside over the state senate, in Massachusetts;
I served on some committees,
functioned as "administrative inspector,"
and when Sam decided not to run in 1918,
I ran unopposed for the nomination.

Channing Cox, a Boston lawyer and Speaker
of the House on Beacon Hill, my running mate,
I barely beat the Democrat, Richard H. Long,
a Framingham businessman,
but when I ran against him for re-election in 1919?
A landslide! It was the last 1-year gubernatorial race.
The term went to two years in 1920.

Mine was a progressive administration—
higher teachers' salaries, women's suffrage,
direct election of senators, labor unions—
but it was my "law and order" policies in 1919
that catapulted me to national attention.

PHILOSOPHICAL INTERLUDE

The Tao According to Cal

"A wise old owl lived in an oak
The more he saw the less he spoke
The less he spoke the more he heard
Why can't we all be like that wise old bird?"

The plaque on my living room wall
on Massasoit Street in Northampton
pretty much summed up my attitude.
How can words ever spell out grief?
How can the word "grief" capture grief?
Or "sorrow" sorrow or "love" love,
"gratitude" gratitude?
Those who know do not talk.
Those who talk do not know.

Silence

> "Many times I say only 'yes' or 'no' to people.
> Even that is too much.
> It winds them up for twenty minutes or more."
> —Coolidge to Bernard Baruch

You have no need to prove yourself.
You don't need to be seen.
Speech is the yang of silence,
silence the yin of speech.

Silence? The transcendence of speech,
not merely its absence.

I know the jokes.
I even find them funny.
"Silent Cal": the nickname makes me smile.
The woman I sat next to at dinner
who told me, "I bet my friend
I would be able to get more
than two words out of you tonight."

"You lose."

Did I really say that?
It makes a good story, doesn't it?

PART TWO

Boston Police Strike

> "Men fought each other, not knowing why they fought."
> —Newspaper reporter

That September the Boston police went on strike.
Labor ran amok, worldwide. The Bolsheviks'd tightened their hold
in Russia. The Spartacus League in Germany not only
claimed the right to strike but to confiscate property.
Ole Hanson faced death threats in Seattle
when he condemned a general strike as "domestic bolshevism,"
quit the job after an assassination attempt.
"I am tired out and going fishing," he declared.
John Lewis of the United Mine Workers called
for a nationwide strike of coal workers.

So when the Boston Police walked out of station houses
that Tuesday, September 9, 1919, nobody knew what to do.
In Roxbury a streetcar conductor was shot in the leg;
ruffians went up and down Washington Street smashing windows;
in Tremont Street, looters broke into small shops.
At Scollay Square, a 70-year-old fruit stand worker
held off a crowd storming a shoe store
while in the North End groups terrorized girls and women.

The Massachusetts State Guard restored order.
I won't get into the political details
with the mayor, police commissioner and President Wilson,
but in the end I declared, "The action of the police
in leaving their posts of duty is not a strike.
It is a desertion."
The men could not return to their jobs. Ever.

Order was restored and though I tried to help the men
find other jobs, they could not return to the police.
I stood firm on the strikers.
All over America, people noticed.

The Strike

I never did care much for Mayor Peters.
He seemed so proud, too certain
of himself, but more like an entitlement
than the confidence of his accomplishment.
A Harvard boy who traced his Boston lineage
back to the seventeenth century.

When the police went on strike,
Peters called up Boston-based state guardsmen,
fired Edwin Curtis, the police commissioner,
neither of which actions he had the authority to do.
These were solely the responsibility of the governor. Me.

I found him at the armory ordering the men about,
and when I told the guardsmen to go home,
Peters flew into a rage.
"But the city is rioting, Governor Coolidge!"

I told him to go home, my tone that of a parent
scolding a child throwing a tantrum.
That's when Peters punched me in the face.
General Stevens and Colonel Dalton restrained him.

"Let him find it out in the papers!"
I snapped at my secretary, William Butler,
when I rescinded Peters' orders, restored Curtis,
though ultimately we transmitted the documents to City Hall—
and Peters grudgingly gave his support.

Later, when Peters was implicated in the murder
of his niece, Starr Faithfull, a girl he'd been rumored
to have sexually abused as a child,
paying her hush money to avoid scandal,
it only confirmed my estimation of him,
guilty or not.

Vice President

When all the Progressives returned to the G.O.P.,
everybody figured TR'd be the nominee for president in 1920,
but then the blood clot killed him, only 60,
after feeling unwell for a January day.
"Put out the light, James," his last words
to his servant. Totally unexpected.
He'd never recovered from his son Quentin's death,
his plane shot down over France on Bastille Day, 1918.
I could only imagine his sorrow over losing his son.

And talk about unexpected,
nobody thought Warren would get the nomination,
tenth ballot, and me?
My name had been floated as a dark horse,
my handling of the Boston police strike
propelling me to national attention.

I didn't *want* to be Vice President,
but Wallace McCamant of Oregon placed my name
at the national convention in Chicago,
and the delegates stampeded my way.
So there I was, Warren's running mate,
the Republican candidate for Vice President, 1920.

President

Warren hadn't been well for a while.
I'd delivered the budget address in his place,
then we bade each other goodbye March 4,
for the long congressional recess.
That was the last time I saw him alive.
Later I heard he'd learned of Forbes' treachery,
what became known as the Teapot Dome scandal,
which surely added to the grief weighing on his heart.
And there was that business with Nan Britton
that came out three or four years after he died,
the young woman who wrote a book,
claimed Warren had fathered her child.

Warren and Florence traveled to Alaska that summer,
I think to get away from it all.
They stopped at the Palace Hotel in San Francisco
en route to Washington, where he died,
a heart attack at age fifty-seven.

We were in Plymouth, Vermont, visiting family
when on the night of August 2, 1923,
my father awakened me with the news,
voice trembling with his emotion.
Father was the first to address me as President,
the culmination of a lifelong desire for my success,
but oh, the circumstances!
He placed in my hands the official report
of President Harding's passing away.

After I dispatched a telegram to Mrs. Harding,
Father, a notary public, administered the oath of office,
swearing me in as President.

Love Child

I'd heard the rumors—who hadn't?
Sex in a White House closet and the rest of it.
Warren had a reputation as a ladies' man.
Florence was five years his senior,
a child by a previous marriage,
and Warren was said to've carried on an affair
with another young woman from Marion, Ohio —
that's where Nan Britton was from, too.
Carrie Fulton Phillips was her name,
the wife of a Marion department store owner;
they said the affair lasted fifteen years, ended in 1920.

In her shocking 1927 book, *The President's Daughter,*
Nan Britton claimed her daughter Elizabeth was Warren's, too.
Britton wasn't even born yet when Warren married Florence,
a quarter century younger than Warren.
As a teenager she'd been smitten by him,
her father'd told Warren, one dad to another.
She moved to New York when she graduated
from high school, worked as a secretary.

Britton lost the paternity lawsuit, having no concrete evidence.
After Congressman Mauser's vicious attacks
during the cross-examination, Britton's case was dead.
I understand she moved to Oregon.
Florence refused to honor Warren's so-called "promise"
to support the child, Elizabeth Ann.

---

* In 2015 Ancestry.com confirmed Harding's paternity based on DNA evidence.

The Progress of a People

I'd addressed Howard University just before
the Republican convention, in 1924,
horrified by the rise of the Ku Klux Klan,
their apogee in early 1920s culminating in the Klan Bake,
the Democratic convention in New York that July.

I never denounced the Klan by name,
but I tried to reassure the communities
living under the threat of KKK violence—
blacks, Catholics, Jews.

I'd already welcomed Robert Russa Moton,
superintendent of Tuskegee, to the White House,
and I appointed William Matthews
National Colored Republican Organizer—
first time in history a presidential campaign
had named a negro to lead the effort.

At Howard I denounced the hideous crime of lynching—
I'd already advocated for passage of the Dyer Anti-Lynching Bill
during my first State of the Union address in December—
praised black patriotism during the recent world war.

"The progress of the colored people on this continent
is one of the marvels of modern history," I observed.
"We are perhaps even yet too near to this phenomenon
to be able to appreciate its significance."

I hope I didn't sound too patronizing.

Leading Eagle

I count Native American blood in my lineage,
on my father's side,
but after poet Ruth Muskrat's impassioned speech
when I invited a group of Native Americans to the White House
(a junior at Mount Holyoke at the time, December of 1923),
my advocacy for the 1924 Indian Citizenship Act only
strengthened.
In 1925 I commemorated its enactment
with tribes from the Plateau region, northwest United States,
including the Shuswap, Lillooet and Nlaka'pamux,
the Coeur d'Alene, Spokan and Flathead peoples.
A month later a delegation of twenty came to the White House,
including three Sioux chiefs, descendants of Sitting Bull.

But it was in 1927, when Grace and I vacationed
in the Black Hills of South Dakota,
staying at the State Game Lodge in Custer State Park—
"the Summer White House"—
that I met with Lakota tribesmen at Deadwood.
Henry Standing Bear and Chauncey Yellow Robe inducted me
into the Lakota tribe, Chauncey's daughter Rosebud presenting me
with a feather bonnet and yellow skins.
After Standing Bear's remarks, Chauncey bestowed
the Lakota name Wanblee-Tokaha on me—
Leading Eagle—while Rosebud placed the head-dress on me.
They also gave moccasins to Grace.

Later I visited a reservation called Pine Ridge.
Black Horn, one of the tribe's elders, led
five hundred Lakota in dancing, singing, playing drums.

True, the Sioux claimed the Black Hills rightfully theirs.
I did not address their claims, though I recognized
all the injustices they have endured.

Appointing the First Federal Female Judge

The nineteenth amendment to the Constitution,
passed in June, 1919, ratified in August, 2020,
may have given women the right to vote,
but it wasn't until May, 1928,
that a woman became a federal judge.

On May 4, I nominated Genevieve Rose Cline
to an Associate Justice seat
on the United States Customs Court,
which had been vacated by William Adamson.
Confirmed by the Senate three weeks later,
she took her oath of office
in the Cleveland Federal Building in June.

It took nearly 140 years after the establishment
of the federal court system to do it, but I did it,
and I am glad I did.

Prosperity

They called it the Roaring Twenties,
war over, a time of unprecedented wealth.
For most of the decade I was president.

What did I do?
Proposed tax cuts.
As I said in my 1925 Inaugural address,
I want the people of America
to be able to work less
for the Government
and more for themselves.

But frankly, what
did I *really* do?
I got out of the way.
I did nothing.

As the Chinese philosopher
Lao Tzu said in the *Tao Te Ching*,
People starve. The rulers consume too much with their taxes.
That is why people starve.
And more Taoist wisdom:
I do not act, and people become reformed by themselves.
I do not interfere, and people become rich by themselves.

The Experimental Farm

Grace and I toured the government-run farm.
A farm boy myself, I was curious.
Grace? Not so much.
But when she was taken to the henhouse,
saw just the one rooster
among all the hens and chicks,
she remarked about it to the farmer,
who boasted about his "prize" rooster,
able to "service" the whole henhouse.

"Just how many times a day does he copulate?"
she asked. The answer? Thirty-five to forty.

"Be sure to tell *that* to President Coolidge
when he passes this way," she smiled.

Half an hour later my escorts and I
passed through the same henhouse.
The farmer passed on Grace's message.

"Hmm, thirty to forty times a day?"
I mused. "Same hen?"

"Oh no," the farmer assured me.
"He services them all."

"Be sure to tell *that* to Mrs. Coolidge," I smiled.

PART THREE

Klan Bake

I'd been nominated for president
just a few weeks earlier, in Cleveland,
at the Republican National Convention,
Charles Dawes my Veep,
after Frank Lowden rejected the nomination,
both men from Illinois.

The Imperial Wizard of the KKK was there,
Hiram Wesley Evans, but
despite *Time* dubbing it "the Kleveland Konvention,"
they kept a low profile, nothing like
the Klan Bake in New York City in July,
the Democratic Party held hostage.

The Klan wielded power at the Democrats' convention,
denouncing the "Papist," Al Smith,
throwing support to Wilson's son-in-law, McAdoo—
Wilson, who'd raised the Klan's profile,
celebrating Griffith's *The Birth of a Nation* at the White House.

I'd given my address at Howard University
only a week before the Cleveland convention,
"The Progress of a People,"
praising negroes for their achievements.

Took the Democrats one hundred and three ballots—
almost three weeks!—
to settle on Davis and Bryan—
William Jennings' brother.

Meanwhile, bigger tragedies at home
distracted me from the Democrats' chaos.

Fathers and Sons

I cherished both my boys,
but Calvin was the very image of my mother,
only thirty-nine when she died.
We'd buried her in March,
Vermont snows blustering around,
me just twelve years old.
Grace and John and Calvin made me feel whole again,
but I doted on Calvin, maybe because
he almost died from empyema when he was five.

We'd josh each other all the time;
he had such a fine dry wit about him,
though since both boys were in Pennsylvania,
at Mercersburg Academy,
we only saw each other during school holidays.
John had just graduated,
accepted at Amherst for the fall, my alma mater.

Though my bookworm boy, Calvin worked
summers in the tobacco fields
outside Northampton, and when I became president
after Warren died, that's where he found out.
The story is another young field hand told Calvin,
if his father was president,
he wouldn't be working in a tobacco field.
"If my father were your father you would,"
my boy shot back.

Why oh why did he not wear socks that day?
I'd just been nominated for president,
Charles Dawes my running mate,
high as a kite in a Vermont spring wind,
the boys playing tennis on the White House lawn.

Well, it was 91 degrees out, I suppose,
and there he was, running around the tennis court,
developed a blister on the third toe of his right foot,
and two days later it was killing him, running
a fever, glands in his groin swollen like plums,
red lines streaking his legs.

We moved him to Walter Reed but by the seventh
he'd developed full-blown sepsis.
I cradled him in my arms, but late that night
he was gone.

And when he went?
The power and the glory of the presidency
went with him.

Favorite Son

No parent admits to having a favorite,
unless one child is despicable,
but it was clear Coolidge's second son
was the one he doted on, and when he died?

Charles Dawes, the 1925 Nobel Peace Prize winner,
only weeks before nominated to run
as Coolidge's Vice President, happened to be
at the White House the night Calvin Jr.'s illness
became unmistakable, his fate sealed,
the book closed. Passing the bedroom,
Dawes saw the boy in great distress, his father
bending to him over his bed.
"I have never witnessed such a look
of agony and despair," Dawes recalled.

The same was true of the pathologist, Doctor John Albert Kolmer.
"It's commonly observed that Coolidge is cold as ice,"
he remarked. "But I saw him in his hour of grief,
and I know quite otherwise: the most touching,
heart-rending experience of my professional career."

The funeral began with a service at the White House,
Calvin Jr's coffin covered in pink and white roses,
then a service in Northampton, and finally,
a burial in Plymouth, Vermont.

"He was a boy of much promise," his father eulogized
in his understated way.

I'm Only Sleeping

    after Lennon and McCartney, "I'm Only Sleeping"

After my son's death—
could it really be? Only a week before
he'd had the vigor of a puppy,
then the blister, then the sepsis—
I started sleeping sixteen hours a day,
eleven at night and a four-hour nap,
lost in the comfort of unconsciousness.

But I still had to function.
I couldn't just stop being president,
much as I'd like to.
In time the pain dulled,
but it never left me,
except sometimes when I slept.

The four years went by like water torture,
one drop at a time:
signing bills (Public Buildings Act) and vetoing them
(McNary-Haugen Farm Relief),
ratifying the Kellogg-Briand Pact,
bestowing the Distinguished Service Cross on Lindbergh,
dedicating Mount Rushmore.

And there were more deaths,
my father's in 1926, Grace's mother in 1929,
after we'd returned to Northampton.
Our beloved collie Rob Roy died, too, in 1928,
even after we'd taken him to Walter Reed,
where Calvin Junior had died four years before,
leaving me more lonely than ever.

The Path Leading Us Home

Five years after Calvin's death,
Grace's poem, "The Open Door,"
appeared in *Good Housekeeping*.
My emotions poured out:
Gratitude, sorrow, love.

It was published just before the wedding
of our older boy John and Florence Trumbull,
daughter of John Harper Trumbull,
governor of Connecticut.

They paid her $250 for the poem.
Grace sent the check on to John and Florence
"to use for something in the new home,
in some way that John's brother
might have chosen were he here."

"You, my son," her poem began,
"Have shown me God."
A lump the size of an apple
swelled in my throat,
remembering him.
"Guide me along the path," she wrote,
"which leads us home."

My Father Dies

"He lived a long life," I'd say,
sometimes adding, "a productive life of service,"
wondering if this would be my obituary, too.

When Father died in March that year, 1926,
just shy of his 83rd birthday,
pneumonia, "the old man's friend,"
it felt like one more rung of the ladder gone missing,
stepping into the blank space of generations.

I remembered his grief when his grandson died,
he an octogenarian who'd endured so much sorrow already,
that same crumbling feeling that I'd had,
behind his stoic demeanor.

Not unlike when Mother died, I remembered,
and I remembered how relieved I'd felt
when he and my stepmother married,
his muted joy, palpable as if it were a public square announcement,
how close the two of us had become,
especially after my sister Abbie passed,
his only daughter;
my guilt after I abandoned him for Amherst.

And I remembered her death, too,
Mrs. Caroline Althea Brown Coolidge,
six years before him, a dozen years younger than he,
the same granite stoicism carved into his face.
Loss after loss after loss.

I remembered and I remembered and I remembered.

Losing Grace in the Black Hills

The newspapers blew it all out of proportion, of course.
The Boston Herald headline read:
"Wife's Long Hike Vexes Coolidge: President Paces Porch
as First Lady Hits 15 Mile Trail."
The Boston Post headline echoed this:
"First Lady Almost Lost; President Worried,
On Point of Forming Search Party
Just as Mrs. Coolidge Returns."
The Boston Globe, not to be left out, ran:
"Wife's Delay Taxes Coolidge's Patience."

Then, a few days later, after the kerfuffle:
"Haley Out as Mrs. Coolidge's Escort,"
a reference to Secret Service agent James Haley,
who'd accompanied Grace on the hike.

And of course there were the rumors,
an illicit alliance between the two.
Nothing could be further from the truth.

Of course I was concerned when she hadn't returned.
Nothing unusual there, right?
She'd said she'd be back in an hour.
After three, I was getting nervous.
They'd left at 9:00 in the morning.
By 2:15 I was frantic, started to form the search party.
Only three years since we'd lost our boy.
But of course the press needed a "scandal."

Grace waltzed back in with Haley,
cheerily greeting me,
"Hello, Papa, sorry to keep you waiting!"
I was livid, but I was also relieved.

Our summer White House in Custer State Park,
me trout-fishing, Grace knitting on the porch:
what could possibly be more idyllic?
What could possibly be more boring to the reporters?
Still nursing a broken heart over my son,
I wanted nothing more than the peace and quiet.

Later, Grace contacted the head of the Secret Service,
without my knowledge, to lobby on Haley's behalf.

Two Gun

My favorite bodyguard?
Had to be Richard James "Two Gun" Hart,
the Bureau of Indian Affairs agent
assigned to protect us in the Black Hills.
A prince of a fellow, if something
of a loose cannon, I later learned.

He never said more than "Morning, Mister President,"
or, "Evening, Missus Coolidge," but his silence concealed
volumes of experience, the ineffability of his knowledge:
a man to admire.

Older brother to Al and Frank Capone,
though he himself was a prohibition agent,
going after the bootleggers,
he'd left home in Brooklyn at sixteen
to join the circus as a roustabout,
changed his name from James Vincenzo Capone
to Richard Hart, after his movie idol,
William S. Hart, star of the silent Westerns.

He'd earned the name "Two Gun" after a series
of successful raids as a prohibition agent,
the same nickname as his matinee idol,
claimed to have served in France during the Great War,
though the Army Department didn't have a record of his service,
and the year we spent the summer in the Dakotas
he was assigned to the Cheyenne River Indian reservation.

Can't say Grace and I slept more peacefully
than we did that summer,
under his care.

Cab Driver

Of all the people to almost run over!
Anybody else, I'd have shrugged an apology,
been on my way back home to Baltimore.

I'd come to the intersection
of H Street and Jackson Place,
maybe took the corner too sharp,
veering in toward the curb,
but I didn't hit him, didn't
even come close to running Coolidge over!

But then the secret service guy,
a different one from the one who grabbed Cal's arm,
jumped onto my running board,
startled the hell out of me.
"Who are you?" I demanded.
"Secret Service!"

He called over to a street cop,
had me arrested, charged me
with cutting corners, failing
to give the right of way to a pedestrian—
who just happened to be the president.
They released me on a $5,500 bond,
for an appearance in traffic court.

Coolidge? He wasn't even bothered
by what the papers called his "narrow escape."
Didn't even tell his staff about it
until he remembered a few hours later.

But of course the newspapers
made a big deal out of it.
To hear them, I practically sent Cal
up in the air all the way back
to the White House, a block away.

It didn't help that his wife Grace,
the First Lady, had almost been hit
by a motorcycle up in Swampscott,
Massachusetts, the summer before.

Robbed of Our Pet

Grace got Rob Roy in 1922,
from Island White Kennels in Oshkosh, Wisconsin,
having fallen in love with collies
after seeing one perform in the circus.

He was my favorite among the menagerie of pets,
even more than his beloved companion,
our red chow, Tiny Tim.
We kept birds, cats, raccoons, other dogs, too,
but Rob Roy was a stately gentleman
of great courage and fidelity;
we all loved him, John, Calvin, Grace and I.

Once, having lunch with Senator Morris Sheppard,
author of the eighteenth amendment,
prohibiting the sale and consumption of alcohol,
Rob nosed his leg, much to Sheppard's annoyance.
But I ordered Sheppard to surrender his sausage.

Howard Christy's portrait of Grace,
originally hung in the Red Room of the White House,
shows the First Lady with Rob Roy,
the dog's devoted gaze directed at Grace—
which we achieved by feeding him candy,
from my hand to his mouth,
throughout the portrait sittings.

Rob Roy especially liked going fishing with me,
riding in the boats, nose in the air, sniffing.
When he became ill in 1928, we took him to Walter Reed,
where our son Calvin had died,
but he, too, could not be saved.

It's the most tragic thing about pets,
how devoted they are to you,
how attached you become to them,
only to watch them suffer and die before you.

I Do Not Choose to Run

I had no intention of running again in 1928.
I thought to get out of the way early
so the party could choose a successor.
As I later said in my autobiography,
the office takes a toll on a person.
I didn't mention my son,
but Calvin's death was always with me,
like a shroud.

So on August 2, 1927—
four years to the day I was sworn in as President,
following Warren's death—
while we were vacationing at the summer White House,
I handed out slips of paper to reporters
in Rapid City, South Dakota, that stated:
"I do not choose to run
for President in nineteen twenty-eight."

Of course, the wags had a field day with it.
Harry Reser's Jazz Band made a recording
about a watch that, instead of telling the time,
repeated my phrase: *I do not choose to run /*
I do not choose to run / try and shake me /
You can't make me / My spring days are done.
Wind me up once more / Then drop me on the floor
No, I don't care / I just declare
I do not choose to run.

Ha ha. Of course there were those who said
I was being intentionally ambiguous,
that I would accept the nomination
if I were drafted,
but I did not want the job.
I thought my simple statement made it clear.
You simply can't persuade the journalists!

Five days later,
along with the Prince of Wales,
I dedicated the Peace Bridge at Niagara Falls.

The Lame Duck

The term originally applied to people in finance.
Horace Walpole first used it in the eighteenth century
in a letter to Sir Horace Mann.

I have the distinction of being the first president
about whom the term was used.
Soon after my term ended?
The Constitution was amended
to shorten the so-called "lame-duck period,"
 moving inaugurations back
from March to January 20,
but that wouldn't happen until 1937.

The lame duck in the wild,
unable to keep up with the flock,
is said to be vulnerable to predators.
I did not then feel threatened,
despite some of the unkind words.

PART FOUR

How Can You Tell?

When my father died,
the story went,
the famous wit, Dorothy Parker,
quipped, "How can you tell?"

This was a joke on his nickname,
"Silent Cal," but did she know
he slept most of the day,
trying to forget?

"If I had not been president," he wrote,
the anguish like a vise squeezing his heart,
"he would not have raised a blister on his toe,
which resulted in blood poisoning,
playing lawn tennis in the South Grounds."

After my brother died,
my father never recovered.
It was like Teddy Roosevelt,
after *his* son Quentin died,
only twenty-one, in France,
during the war.

If only you could take it back!
But you can't; you have to live with it.
My Father's sorrow and suffering never left him—
except sometimes in the oblivion of sleep.

Mark of Cain

Though tenderhearted,
Father kept his feelings to himself,
the stoic New Englander,
but after the White House service,
when they bore my brother's casket to the hearse,
he broke down and wept,
the first time I'd ever seen him cry.

It felt like time had stopped,
an eternal tableau of pure mourning,
as if father were Adam,
the first man to lose a son.

Did this make me Cain?
Calvin was my father's favorite.
I felt responsible, as if
I'd somehow been negligent
when we were playing tennis.

Did he complain about his foot?
I don't remember, but in my dreams
I hear him asking me if he should stop.
Sometimes I say yes, sometimes no.
Did I harbor thoughts of fratricide,
a latter-day Cain,
jealous of our father's love?

Calvin's death hurt him terribly.
It hurt us all. Terribly.

Daddy Death

Only sixty when he died,
fewer than four years since leaving office—
not quite nine since Calvin's death—
Father's heartbreak followed him
like a sinister shadow,
dragging him to the grave.
How gaunt he looked!
He made me think of Yorick,
the skull in the graveyard, not the jester.

Back at The Beeches, his Northampton home,
he'd commented to his secretary, Harry Ross,
only the day before he died,
that he was getting to be an old man;
perhaps he might just stop going
down to the office every day, he speculated.
He'd complained about slight attacks
of indigestion, but he didn't call the doctor.

Mid-morning on the fifth of January,
his heart gave out—a coronary thrombosis—
while he shaved. ("Heart attack" sounds so prosaic!)

Ross told us Father'd gone to the office
around 8;30 but only stayed a little over an hour,
telling Ross around 10:00,
"Well, I guess we'll go up to the house."

At The Beeches, he sat in his study,
reading the morning newspapers,
when Mother came in to tell him
she was walking into town to do her shopping.

"Don't you want the car?" he asked her.

"No," she said. "It's such a nice day.
I'd rather walk than ride."

Those were their last words to each other.

Daddy Burial

We buried him beside Calvin Jr.,
in the family plot, Plymouth Notch Cemetery.
We'd put mother there beside them
when she passed a quarter century later, in 1957.

Mother kept the funeral simple, no eulogy,
no official observance in Washington or Boston.
Instead, the funeral was held at the Edwards Congregational
 Church
in Northampton, the burial in Plymouth Notch,
two days after he died, January 7.

A train from Washington brought President Hoover, his wife Lou,
Vice President Curtis and Chief Justice Hughes to Northampton.
President-elect Roosevelt sent his son James and wife Eleanor,
so three first ladies attended the service in Edwards Church.

The casket containing father's body was driven from The Beeches
to Edwards around 8:00 in the morning.
An honor guard of Northampton police carried the body into the
 church,
where it lay in state with a two-man honor guard.
At 8:30 they opened the doors and the public was permitted
to file past the casket, paying final respects to "Cal."
They closed the door an hour later, hundreds still outside,
denied a final glimpse of my father.

An organist played three pieces: Handel's *Xerxes,*
Chopin's funeral march, and the largo
from Dvorak's *New World Symphony.*
The service lasted just twenty minutes.

The Washington entourage came back to the Beeches
to pay their final respects to Mother,
then returned to the depot to board the train back to DC.
Mother and the family joined the cortege
to bring Father's remains to Vermont, up Route Five
through South Deerfield, Greenfield and Brattleboro.
At the state line, the Vermont State Police took over
the escort duties, making our way to the cemetery
where Father was buried with his family and ancestors.

Guardian

I'd spend my life in business,
a railroad executive,
with the New York, New Haven and Hartford Railroad,
later president of the Connecticut Manifold Forms Company.

I met my wife Florence, daughter
of Governor Trumbull of Connecticut,
on a train bound for Washington in 1925,
on my way to Father's inauguration.
We settled in Connecticut after marrying in 1929.

We named our first daughter Cynthia,
conceived two months after Father's death,
her name preserving Father's initials, CC.

In 1960, at the age of 54,
three years after Mother died,
I reopened the Plymouth Cheese Corporation
back in Plymouth Notch, Vermont,
using 19th-century methods to make cheese,
part of an effort to preserve the town
where Father was born and sworn in as president,
helping start the Coolidge Foundation,
donating land and buildings to create
the President Calvin Coolidge State Historic Site,
self-appointed guardian of Father's legacy.

In This Silence Discover Yourself

Like my father, I'm a man of few words.
Was he a good president? I defend him,
but I leave that to the historians.
I do know that he was a good man.

Walter Lippmann, the columnist and pundit,
once charged that my father possessed
a veritable "genius for inactivity."
H.L. Mencken said Father was
"as appalling and fascinating as a two-headed boy."
If the Depression had occurred during his administration,
"he would have responded to bad times
precisely as he responded to good ones—
pulling down the blinds, stretching his legs upon his desk,
snoozing away the lazy afternoons.
He slept more than any other President,
whether by day or by night.
Nero fiddled, but Coolidge only snored."
Yes, some have said his policies led
to the Great Depression that fell like an anvil
half a year into Herbert Hoover's administration.

"The business of America is business,"
often attributed to Father, but what he actually said
in a 1925 speech to newspaper reporters was
"The chief business of the American people is business."
He went on to say Americans were concerned
with "producing, buying, selling, investing and prospering."

I often wondered if Mother's experience with the deaf
at the Clarke School didn't somehow figure
into her attraction to Father,
living with all that silence in your head.

After Father died, Mother became
Chairman of the Board at Clarke School,
where she served until 1952.

I think of the quotations from Lao Tzu's *Tao Te Ching:*
To be of few words is natural.
Peace and quiet govern the world.
I do not act, and people become reformed by themselves.
I am at peace, and people become fair by themselves.

The First Lady of Baseball

During her time in the White House,
Mother rooted for the Washington Senators,
became known as "the First Lady of Baseball."
"You may not give a hoot for the sport,"
she told her friends, "but to me,
it is my very life."

The American League sent her a yearly pass
sealed in a gold-trimmed purse.

Bucky Harris, the Senators' manager, called her
"the most rabid baseball fan I ever knew
in the White House." The Coolidges attended
Harris' wedding in October, 1926.

Mother attended as many games as she could,
faithfully filling out her scorecard,
and when they were on The Mayflower,
the presidential yacht, sailing down the Potomac,
she tuned in the Senators' games on station WRC.

When the Senators clinched the pennant in 1924,
Mother and Father attended the first game,
the World Series starting in Griffith Stadium,
Walter Johnson, 36, on the mound.
I was just starting at Amherst, my brother,
Calvin Jr., only three months dead.

The score tied 2-2 after nine innings,
Father got up to leave. Mother, wearing her
"good luck" necklace, seven ivory elephants,
 yanked him back into his seat. She snapped,
"Where do you think you're going?"
Father sat back down to watch
the Giants win 4-3 in twelve.

The Senators won the series in seven,
another nail-biting twelve-inning game,
Johnson getting the final win in relief,
though he'd lost the two games he started.
Exultant fans carried him to the President,
who said in his characteristic understated way,
"Nice work. I'm glad you won."
But mother? She jumped for joy!

Just a White House Conversation

Regular parishioners
of the First Congregational Church,
with its long tradition of commitment
to the social gospels principle,
we'd just come back from Sunday services.
Not feeling well that morning,
Mother had not been able to attend.
She asked us about the service.

Mother: "What was the sermon about?"
Father: "Sin."
Mother: "What did he say?"
Father: "He was against it."

The Return of Two Gun

Though there seemed some private dispute
between Father and Mother,
whenever they spoke of Agent Hedges,
the agent with Mother when she "got lost"
in the Black Hills—
the usual Coolidge wordless argument;
Father who rarely spoke anyway,
Mother attuned to the depths of the deaf—
they were in agreement about "Two Gun" Hart,
the Bureau of Indian Affairs man,
an upright fellow, likewise laconic,
kept his private thoughts to himself.

Years later, after Father had died,
I learned Two Gun had returned to Homer, Nebraska,
as a prohibition agent,
where he busted bootleggers on Indian reservations,
until he was convicted of manslaughter
for killing a wanted man who refused to surrender.

After Prohibition ended, he became a marshal
and a justice of the peace, in Homer,
but he was dismissed after being caught shoplifting
from a local grocery store.

Subpoenaed to testify before a Grand Jury in Chicago,
a tax evasion trial involving his brother Ralph,
he'd hobbled into the courtroom on a cane.
Suffering from diabetes, Two Gun had a heart attack

shortly after testifying, buried back in Homer, where his wife and four children lived.

I think Father would have been amused.

Back in Northampton

Mother lived almost a quarter century
after her husband died.
They'd bought The Beeches in Northampton,
a gated estate on Hampton Court,
though they had planned to move
back to Massasoit Street after retirement,
where we'd lived since 1906,
but it just didn't offer the privacy they needed.
She'd later sell The Beeches and build
Road Forks, on Ward Avenue,
which she loaned to the WAVES in World War II.

After they moved back to Northampton,
Mother plunged into community service.
She did local charity work for the Red Cross,
raised funds to help refugee children in Germany,
raised money for the Queen Wilhelmina Fund
for the Dutch victims of the Nazi invaders.

Perhaps because she'd had curvature of the spine
as a young woman, overcame it through exercise,
she had a special interest in people with disabilities,
sought them out to visit the White House.
It's why she'd taught at the Clarke School for the Deaf,
later chairman of the Board for twenty years.
Mother invited Helen Keller to the White House.

She received an honorary doctorate from Smith,
another from the University of Vermont.

Mother's good friend, Ivah W. Gale from Newport, Vermont,
lived with Mother at Road Forks, her final years.
Ivah'd lived with the Goodhues, Mother's parents,
when they were in college at UVM, a lifelong friend.
"She is more like a sister than any other friend I have."

The Precious Four

Mother called me and Florence and our daughters,
Cynthia and Lydia, her "precious four."

It had nothing to do with the four most precious gemstones,
diamonds, rubies, sapphires and emeralds,
but everything to do with love of family.
As the *Tao Te Ching* puts it,
"Cultivate virtue in the family, and it will be overflowing."

After I took the job with the railroad,
we lived in Westville, Connecticut.
Later, we moved to Orange.
Mother visited us often, as we did her.

Just before our wedding, Mother had written,
"John, you are a son for a mother
to be proud of, and I want you
to always feel that I am standing by,
ready to do anything for you and Florence."

And thus it was.
After Father died,
we became even closer;
our fondness for Father grew, too,
as his strictness faded from memory.

Thousands of Questions by Hundreds of Reporters

Hoover'd been nominated in June,
after Father'd made it clear
he wasn't running again.

I'd just graduated from Amherst,
decided to get into the railroad business,
after talking about it with Father.

Mother knew I'd be hounded by journalists
after she packed my bags on Labor Day
before I boarded the train to Chicago.

Did those reporters hound me!
They wanted to know about my engagement
with Florence Trumbull,
a possible White House wedding.

"I have nothing to say. I have nothing to say,"
I kept telling them at Union Station,
but they still noted the two battered old felt hats
on the outside of my suitcase
when I passed through Manhattan.
What a thing to report!

Florence had been away overseas,
but I didn't dare meet her
when the S.S. Lapland docked in Manhattan.

The reporters hounded Florence as well.
As she debarked from the S.S. Lapland,
she informed them that she and I
had "our own understanding," telling them
we would not be wed before Christmas.
A White House wedding would be "thrilling,"
she said, "but there isn't much chance of that."

Calvin Coolidge Put Together

My favorite Calvin Coolidge joke?
It has to be from that 1952 Gene Kelly movie,
Singin' in the Rain, when Lina Lamont,
played by Jean Hagen, declares,
"I make more money than Calvin Coolidge!"
then splutters, "put together!"

A nostalgic movie about talkies,
which replaced silent films during
Father's years in office. *The Jazz Singer,*
with Al Jolson, premiered in 1927.

In fact, God's honest truth,
Father was the first president
to appear in a talkie, a recording
of one of his speeches.

I remember Father liked to make people laugh
with the lean, dry wit that punctuated his silence,
that famous New England laconic stoicism—
why he preferred my brother to me, maybe,
the brand of humor they shared.

In formal addresses he was super-serious, dignified,
you might even say *boring.*
But Father was as high-minded as they come,
and I admired him for it, even though
he always made us dress for dinner.

Fortinbras Rhymes with FDR

As far as sons go,
I think I am more Fortinbras than Hamlet—
more decisive and confident.
I spent my life making business decisions,
establishing the Coolidge Foundation,
the President Calvin Coolidge State Historic Site.

The Calvin Coolidge House on Massasoit Street
in Northampton, where I grew up, added
to the National Register of Historic Places in 1976.

It occurs to me that "Fortinbras" sounds
a little like "FDR."
Fortinbras—"strength in arms"—
the savior of Norway in the end.
And FDR? A lifelong Republican,
I never voted for the man once.
But I grudgingly admired his efforts
to bring us out of the Great Depression.

Father never much liked Herbert Hoover.
He thought he boasted too much,
mockingly called him "Wonder Boy."
"That man," he once said, "has offered me
unsolicited advice every day for six years,
most of it bad."

Still, he endorsed his Commerce secretary
when Hoover ran in 1928.

"Let four captains bear Hamlet like a soldier
to the stage," Fortinbras says. "For he was likely,
had he been put upon, to have proved most royally."
Easy to say when your rival is dead.

The Good Die Young

Turns out Abraham Lincoln's only grandson,
Abraham "Jack" Lincoln II,
also died from blood poisoning,
likewise at the age of sixteen,
in Paris in 1890 after minor surgery,
a lanced carbuncle that'd developed under his arm,
and then the sepsis set in.
The son of Robert Todd Lincoln and his wife Mary Eunice.

And of course Lincoln's own boy, Willie,
died at the age of eleven, 1862, typhoid fever,
his parents inconsolable, Abe bursting into tears
not unlike my own father.

Teddy Roosevelt's son died in France
during the Great War, Quentin shot down
in aerial combat, his father out of office by then
but still a political force in the Republican party.

Nor can I forget Patrick Kennedy, born
three weeks early, dead after three days' life,
respiratory distress syndrome,
just three months before his father was assassinated, 1963.

But none of this ever eases the grief, does it?
Losing my brother
left such a huge hole in my soul.

The Rest Is Silence

Well, I've eked into the new millennium,
93 years old, though it's lonely without Florence.
Married 69 years before she passed on
 a couple of years ago, likewise at age 93,
she born November 30, 1904,
me September 7, 1906.
She's buried by my parents and brother
in the Plymouth Notch Cemetery.
I'll be joining her before too much longer.

I think of Father's silence, a trait
I always tried to emulate, as it enhances
self-control, self-awareness, spirituality,
enables you to have some perspective.

Those of us close to him
knew he'd never recovered
from my brother's death.
Did he welcome his own,
that ultimate silence?

Blessed silence, blessed peace.
And I likewise wonder,
did Hamlet long for death?
Is that the meaning of his final speech?

As he lay dying, Hamlet says to Horatio—
Gertrude, his mother, Claudius and Laertes
all dead around him, a grisly tableau—
"The rest is silence."

ENVOI

Bard

I like to think of the barred owl
as the "bard" owl,
sage poet of the forest,
mask face ancient as a totem pole,
expressively expressionless expression,
omniscience made flesh and feathers.

WHO who who-who it calls
("who cooks for you" the mnemonic,
but I hear an accusation, a summons:
YOU You you-you . . .).

In the pre-dawn quiet of the woods
its prophetic warning clear as Gabriel,
the silence that follows deafening,
until a sudden screech pierces the dark,
a small rodent, the bard's prey;
then the silence comes roaring back.

About the Author

Charles Rammelkamp lives in Baltimore, Maryland, with his wife, Abby, where he writes poetry and fiction. Recent works include the poetry collections, *See What I Mean?* (Kelsay Books, 2023) and *The Trapeze of Your Flesh* (BlazeVOX, 2024).

Rammelkamp is Prose Editor for Brickhouse Books, the longest continuously publishing literary publisher in Maryland, and he writes reviews for *North of Oxford, The Lake,* and several other journals.

www.ingramcontent.com/pod-product-compliance
Lightning Source LLC
Chambersburg PA
CBHW072049160426
43197CB00014B/2694